WORLD EMPIRE

Bible Prophecy and the European Union II

ERIKA GREY

Pedante Press

Sequel to the Seat of the Antichrist: Bible Prophecy and the European Union

This work provides the second part to the Seat of the Antichrist and updates it from March 2010 until the present.

All Scriptural quotations in this publication are from the New King James Version of the Bible © by Thomas Nelson, Inc.

DEDICATION

To you dad who made this work possible.

CONTENTS

www.erikagrey.com

For Bible Prophecy news and analysis and more books visit my website.

1
SIGNS OF THE TIMES

The world has been experiencing a level of violence unseen within the last couple of decades. ISIS emerged in 2011 and shocked with world with its horrific savage images. They proudly shared their beheadings in videos around the world. Between 2013 and 2014 the world witnessed the most horrific images to come from any one war.

Gay Marriage Goes Global

In 2015 gay marriage was legalized in the United States and this movement and laws swept the Western world. Birth Certificate's changed to reflect absurd genders. The world has drawn away from male and female as God created them. Small children even voice their sex as the opposite of what they are born. Transgender has become a common word in the English vocabulary.

Mass Shootings

Mass shootings marked the decade with the Sandy Hook murders of December 13, 2012, shocking the world. Never had anyone gone into a school with young children between six and seven years old and massacred them in such a brutal and viscous manner. Adam Lanza killed 26 people that day including his own mother. Afterwards random shootings have now become a regular occurrence and deadlier.

1000-man gang Crime Spree

In 2016, a 1000-man gang that "went on a crime spree on New Year's Eve sexually assaulting, robbing and even raping women in the City of Cologne, according to Alex Griswold of Media ITE. German police denounced what they called 'a completely new dimension of crime.'" The Washington Post reported an even greater number. They stated that "a leaked document says 2,000 men allegedly assaulted 1,200 German women on New Year's Eve. This event too was unprecedented and marks an evil era.

Social Ills Escalate

All kinds of social ills run rampant, from a rise in obesity which even effects children. Even in India obesity is rising faster than the world average. In addition to gluttony the rates of drug abuse deaths and suicide has also skyrocketed. In one day in New Haven CT 70 people overdosed. Social unrest is also climbing. Rioting increased and the BLM protests of 2020 went global.

Among the social ills were bazaar experiments in science. The discovery of Crispr cas9 allows scientists to alter DNA. Gene editing produced testing that was straight out of a science fiction movie. In 2013 in Canada goats were on display that were engineered with spider DNA. The idea was to create silk that can be extracted from their milk to make textiles such as bulletproof vests. It was called, BioSteel. On Demand News reported that same year that scientists created rabbits that glow in the dark using jellyfish DNA.

In 2019 the company ODIN made gene editing kits for use in the classroom. Instead of dissecting frogs they would experiment and recreate them. At its inception Phys.Org reported that "biologist's gene-editing kit lets do-it-yourselfers play God at the kitchen table.

Diseases and Pandemics

Over this past several years have been many disease scares. Ebola had a domino effect in 2013. Other mosquito and tick born illnesses came on the scene. Each with horrific effects on the human body that are straight out of a horror film. All of these paled in comparison to the COVID-19 Pandemic. This shook the world because it both spread globally and mutated into different variants.

While this plague acted as another major sign of the times that Jesus said would occur, it also became a source for many false teachings in Evangelical circles. From it originating as part of a conspiracy, to the vaccine as the mark of the beast, all took away from the plague as a retold warning from God Himself. Even on the heels of COVID-19 the monkey virus with all its horrific images emerged on the scene.

Extreme Weather

The weather patterns are so severe this last decade that they signified to Bible prophecy watchers' ample evidence of being in the end times. The term "extreme weather" became commonplace. Weather terms never used before entered the English vocabulary to describe the record breaking events. Shocking images of floods and other natural disasters make regular headlines. These events rose insurance rates and effected homeowners in high-risk states and locations. The rebuilding needed afterwards also stresses government's budgets. As a result, nations took up the torch for climate change.

Moreover, Climate Change became the rallying cry for European Union law and policy this past decade. More so than in any other empire.

The Empire Rises in Unison With Extreme Weather

Strangely the European Union empire is rising in unison with the wickedness in society and the signs in nature. In addition, it is becoming apparent that the weather patterns are leading up to the great famine of Revelation 6. Moreover, we should not be surprised that Climate Change policy leads people away from seeing the extreme weather as a sign of the end times from God Himself. Finally, it has become evident that Climate laws will be a platform the Antichrist will champion. He will shift the focus of the extreme events as coming from God to the idea that they are manmade and that he can offer a solution through regulation.

2

CRISES OF OPPORTUNITY

Meanwhile the European Union experienced many crises. The media reported over and over that the EU was going to fall apart in each of them. On the contrary the empire only continued to move forward. It became apparent that the EU is in the Julius Caesar stage of the Revived Roman Empire. This was the time of the great power's roots, which evolved it into the Roman Empire under Augustus.

European Sovereign Debt Crisis

The European Sovereign Debt crisis which began in 2008 with the collapse of Iceland's banking system and spread to Portugal, Italy,

Ireland, Greece, and Spain in 2009, peaked between 2010 to 2012. The Commission President at the time said he was going to present a green paper on euro stability bonds that would according to Politico EU's article "Barroso says Eurobonds will 'be seen as natural', published November 16, 2011, "present and assess the options for the joint issuance of bonds: by eurozone member states…. Issuing a joint Eurobond would allow countries to obtain financing from the financial markets at a lower interest rate than if they were selling just their own bonds."

The Green paper was drawn up by the Five German wise men of the German economy, a council of economic experts that has been advising German policy makers since 1963.

These would be akin to US treasuries. Although Angela Merkel and Commission president wanted to further strengthen the euro before these would be issued. Greece faced sovereign default in 2015 and with it came countless media articles stating that the euro and the European Union was going to fall apart. I wrote an in April of 2015 stating that Greece would not exit the euro and would remain in the European Union.

The EU's sovereign debt crisis caused the EU to further tighten its ship fiscally and enact as many changes as possible short of a treaty change. These changes include:

Six Pack
Two Pack
The Stability and Growth Pact
Macroeconomic surveillance in the euro area
Treaty on Stability and Coordination and Governance in the Economic and Monetary Union
European Stability Mechanism ESM
The Banking Union

Banking Union

In summary the euro fixes include regulations at the EU level that coordinated fiscal policy among the member nations and put in mechanisms to police them. The Banking Union regulated EU banks so that they would not be governed at the EU level and provide depositor protection and rules for failing banks. These would be supervised by the European Central Bank. A single rule book was drafted, and a single resolution board established. Basically, the EU's Banking Union mirrors the United States. It began functioning on January 1, 2015.

The third pillar of the banking union is a European deposit insurance scheme. This coverage will appl to all banks regardless of their location within the EU. This piece has not been completed.

This EU's Sovereign Debt crisis strengthened the euro. The next pieces on the agenda are the Capital Market's Union and the completion of the Banking Union, which will most likely knock the dollar's dominance out of first place and replace it with the Euro. The Capital Market's Union will basically mirror the United States regulations and system, with an index modeled on the S & P 500 that lists the top performing EU companies.

Revelation 6:6, predicts the great famine and mentions the Roman currency. It states, "a measure of wheat for a denarius." Scripture references this currency because during the Tribulation the euro which is the modern denarius will be the world currency.

On the heels of the Sovereign Debt crisis came the possibility of the collapse of the

Italian banks in 2016. Their destruction did not occur.

EU's Migrant Crisis

Between the years 2015 to 2017 the EU faced another major debacle, its migrant crisis. Also known as the Syrian refugee crisis about 1.3 million people came to Europe requesting asylum. In addition to Syrians came Afghans, Nigerians, Pakistanis, Iraqis, Eritreans, and migrants from the Balkans. These came due to the conflicts and wars in their countries.

There were three routes chosen: the Eastern Mediterranean route, the Western Mediterranean route and the Western African route. This presented the European Union with another emergency and with it more reforms and the building of its empire. Frontex was established in 2004 as the European Agency for the Management of Operational Cooperation at the External Borders, its task was mainly coordinating border control efforts. In 2015 the EU Commission extended its mandate to be a fully-fledged European Border and Coast Guard Agency. It was officially launched in October 2016. In April 2019, MEPs approved 10,000 extra border officers. In addition, on September 2020 the Commission proposed a new pact on migration and asylum which is an EU Common Asylum and Migration Policy.

Belarus

After the upheaval in Belarus, Lukashenko facilitated the transit of migrants toward the EU. It was said the migrants were being weaponized. At the European Council of 24-25 June 2021, EU leaders condemned any attempt by third countries to instrumentalize migrants for political purposes. On 22 October 2021, they said that the EU will continue countering the ongoing hybrid attack launched by the Belarusian regime, including by adopting further restrictive measures against persons and legal entities.

Brexit

In June 2016 the UK voted to leave the European Union. The media once again said that the EU would fail as a result and other nations will follow. The divorce process took some time. On January 31 2020 the departure was final. Much to everyone's surprise, there were no ill effects on the European Union.

Rather the consensus among economists is that in the long term it would negatively affect the UK's economy. In place of its membership the UK signed a free trade agreement with the European Union. It took eight months of negotiations to agree on the pact.

The next EU crisis was COVID-19 which also effected the entire world. Following the Pandemic, the Russia Ukraine war. Both would transform the EU, which is written about in chapter nine.

.

3

ROAD TO MARK OF THE BEAST

This past decade the European Union resolved to win the technological race. In 2014 the EU funded the largest ever program for research and innovation to help accomplish this aim. The European Union Framework Programme's cover five-year periods or money's allocated for research and technological development. From 2002 until 2013 ran projects with small budgets. The Seventh program which ran from 2007 to 2013 increased the budget over three-fold to around 50 billion euros.

Horizon 2020

In 2014 the EU launched the eighth

framework program and the largest named Horizon 2020. It was budgeted a whopping 77 billion euros. It ran from 2014 to 2020. It is followed by the ninth program Horizon Europe which runs from 2021 to 2027, with an even greater 95.5 billion euros. It adds for Climate Change. Horizon 2020 promises breakthroughs, discoveries, and world firsts because it provides the funding for scientists.

European Innovation Council

In March 2021 the European Innovation Council was launched under Horizon Europe It has a budget of €10.1 billion. It supports game changing innovations from early-stage research to proof of concept, technology transfer, and the financing and scale up of start-ups and SMEs. With these ambitious programs that have taken the place of previous ones, the EU is going to come to the development of the Mark of the Beast. It is in this environment that the Mark of the Beast will be discovered and launched.

The Commissioner for Science-The Path

Not only is the money and framework in

place for the discovery of the Mark of the Beast, but so is the roadmap or path for the Antichrist to obtain it. The Commission presidency has a team of commissioners that it appoints who report to the president. As a reminder it is this presidency that is the Seat of the Antichrist. It gives him all the required powers to fulfill the predictions in Scripture. One of the team is the Commissioner for Research, Science, and Innovation.

The European Union's Commissioner for Science and Research's reports to the Commission president, which in the future will be the Antichrist and his responsibilities are as follows:

Making sure that research funding programs, notably Horizon 2020, contribute to the Commission's jobs, growth, and investment package.

Scientists submit a proposal for their research project, and it is evaluated by the Commission, if the Commission likes the project it draws up a grant agreement with the participant. The European Commission then draws up a grant agreement with each participant. The grant agreement confirms what research & innovation activities will be undertaken, the project duration, budget, rates and costs, European Commission's contribution, all rights and obligations and more.

FET: Future and Emerging Technologies

Underneath the Horizon 2020 program is FET. The EU's Future and Emerging Technologies program allocates considerable funding with the mission of turning science into products and it takes the lead in yet uncharted technological territories.

The EU Commission's website it states:

"FET actions are expected to initiate radically new lines of technology through unexplored collaborations between advanced multidisciplinary science and cutting-edge engineering. It will help Europe grasp leadership early on in those promising future technology areas able to renew the basis for future European competitiveness and growth, and that can make a difference for society in the decades to come."

FET Open funds projects on new ideas for radically new future technologies, at an early stage when there are few researchers working on a project topic. FET also nurtures, supports, and helps build exploratory research topics.

The description of the types of projects that FET funds describe the image and mark of the Beast type of technologies. The EU is pouring considerable moneys into these ventures to ensure their success.

FET Flagships are 1-billion, 10-years initiatives, which bring together hundreds of excellent European researchers to unite forces and focus on solving ambitious scientific and technological challenges, such as the Human Brain Project, which started in 2013 and the initiative in Quantum Technology, which began in 2018.

The reason for the huge amount of funding into quantum technologies is in their own words to "ensure Europe's leading role in a technological revolution now under way."

The EU Commission launched its €1 billion flagship-scale initiative in quantum technology, within the H2020 research and innovation framework programme discussed earlier in this report. The "initiative aims to place Europe at the forefront of the second quantum revolution now unfolding worldwide, bringing transformative advances to science, industry and society, and thus securing the EU's position in the world.

Therefore, the spending and infrastructure for the research and development of new technologies is all in place as is the quest to be the empire that makes the discovery and is the first to distribute the product. It will accomplish more than all of this, the technology will provide the Antichrist with his mark for all of society.

The Commissioner's Tasks

The Commissioner for Science and Research oversees Horizon 2020 to make sure the selected projects lead to the EU's economic growth. He also promotes the international excellence of the EU's research and science, and he helps strengthen research capacities and innovation across all Member States. In addition, the Commissioner evaluates how EU-funded research can be used more effectively. He ensures that Commission proposals are based on scientific evidence.

According to the Commission's own wording, "He also encourages private companies to apply research to meet challenges faced by society and create more high-quality jobs. "This means that under the Antichrist he will have the ability to influence the "Mark of the Beast" technology.

Other Duties of the Commissioner

The Commission also states of the duties of the Commissioner:

"The Commissioner is also responsible for establishing strong coordination across the Commission regarding research, science, and innovation matters, to make sure that Commission proposals and activities are based on sound scientific evidence and contribute best to jobs and growth agenda. He is supported by a Directorate-General for Research and Innovation (RTD) and he or she reports to the Commissioner for Research, Science, and Innovation."

Joint Research Center's Role

In addition to the Commissioner for Science and Research's role, The Joint Research Centre, under the responsibility of Commissioner for Education, Culture, Youth and Sport, is the European Commission's science service.

Its mission is to support EU policies and the JRC provides independent scientific and technical advice to the European Commission to support a wide range of European Union policies, and it will also assist in the 'Mark of the Beast' technology and its implementation.

The JRC also maximizes the value of the Horizon programs, which are the biggest EU Research and Innovation programs ever that promises more breakthroughs, discoveries, and world-firsts by taking great ideas from the lab to the market.

The Path to the Mark of the Beast is in Place

Therefore, in this last decade the EU has made leaps in laying the groundwork for the discovery and implementation of the Mark of the Beast. Their current institutional structure with no further changes in those bodies is complete. It is noteworthy that it already exists without further evolution of the EU. The only piece missing is the image and Mark of the Beast. Those discoveries will be found within these programs. The scientists are already on the path to find them. The Antichrist as head of the Commission will be given reports by his commissioner. He will have direct input into their development and implementation. This shows how close we are to the start of the Tribulation.

4

WHORE OF BABYLON

On June 19, 2021, the Catholic News Agency reported that Pope Francis declared venerable the French statesman Robert Schuman, known as a key "founding father" of the European Union. According to the Courtney Mares Rome Correspondent for the agency:

:

Pope Francis spoke highly of Robert Schuman in a letter signed on Oct. 22, encouraging Europeans to "rediscover the path of fraternity that inspired and guided the founders of modern Europe, beginning precisely with Robert Schuman."

St. John Paul II also praised Schuman in 2003 for spending his political life "in the service of the fundamental values of freedom and solidarity, understood fully in the light of the Gospel."

Roman Empire Continues in Catholic Church

Pope Francis has wholly endorsed the European Union, and the papacy views the Union as an extension of the Church. In 2018 I had the honor to correspond with and eventually meet and interview in Paris, Count Christian d'Andlau who had been the former secretary general of Paneuropa. He is currently its president in Strasbourg.

Paneuropa is a think tank that works along with the EU Parliament's political parties. It is especially strong in the EPP The European People's Party. He was given the mantle by the now diseased Archduke Otto Von Hapsburg who served as an MEP within the EPP.

Christian d'Andlau stated to me that he is convinced that the Roman Empire never disappeared but was conveniently continued in the Roman Catholic church.

Furthermore, during our interviews, he

informed me that not only was Otto Von Hapsburg responsible for bringing the Eastern bloc nations into the European Union, but he also lent Paneuropa a Catholic influence within the EU Parliament. His parents were very devout Catholics like himself, and his father was beautified by the Catholic Church as Blessed Karl von Hapsburg. Father George W. Rutler wrote this of him in CERC the Catholic Education Resource Center:

Blessed Charles

Blessed Charles, beatified by Pope John Paul II, whose father had served under him and who bore the Emperor's name, was shocked to inherit the imperial throne, as he was remote in the line of succession. It was the worst time in history, and by the end of the First World War more than half of his fellow countrymen had died in battle. In his brief two years of reign, Charles instituted many reforms of the army and the nation, even using imperial carriages to transport food and fuel to the poor, modeling himself after the social teachings of Pope Leo XIII.

His love was boundless for his wife, the Empress Zita, whom he told on the day after their glittering wedding, "Now we must help each other to get to Heaven." His feast day is not on the anniversary of his death or birth, but on the anniversary of their wedding…. The young father was reluctant to let his eldest son Otto, who would be a principal figure in the collapse of European Communism, watch him die, but said that he must see how a Christian king goes to God.

Thus, we see the Catholic Church identifying with statesman and kings and viewing political endeavors as a protraction of the Catholic Church.

Pope Francis Speaks To EU Parliament

This recent decade the intertwining of the Catholic Church or Whore of Babylon within the European Union also became clear when Pope Francis spoke to the European Parliament on November 24, 2014. The Pope was invited by then EU Parliament President Martin Schulz, on behalf of the European Parliament. This was the first visit to the Parliament by a sovereign pontiff in 26 years. Last time was in 1988, when Pope Jean Paul II delivered an address to Parliament, just one year before the fall of the Berlin Wall.

Opening the formal sitting, Parliament's President Martin Schulz said that the loss of confidence of people in politics, both at national and European level, is "tremendous", stressing that no institution can operate if it lacks support. " We therefore all need to cooperate to regain this lost trust," he said.

Common Goals of EU and Catholic Church

Mr. Schulz stressed the "common goals" of the EU and the Catholic church in promoting "the values of tolerance, respect, equality, solidarity and peace". He further stated that "The European Union is about inclusion and cooperation rather than exclusion and confrontation." Safeguarding human dignity was a key theme of the formal address delivered by Pope Francis to Members of the European Parliament.

He also spoke about Immigration, protecting the environment, and promoting human rights and democracy. Pope Francis urged "Europe to rediscover the best of itself and stated that, "Building a global community is also an international responsibility."

Pope Sees EU as a Success

According to Matteo Gorgoni's article "World Federalism in Pop Francis' Latest Encyclical "Fratelli Tutti," published December 11, 2020, in *Democracy Without Borders:*

"A common denominator can also be found in the secular notion of "global citizenship", which is conceptually promoted in pope Francis' encyclical. As the pontiff says: "To care for the world in which we live means to care for ourselves. "The pontiff recalls that successful prototypes can be found in the European Union and many other regional integration models. …"

Family of Nations

Gorgoni quoted the Pope who stated:

"We talk about the possibility of some form of world authority regulated by law, we need not necessarily think of a personal authority. Still, such an authority ought at least to promote more effective world organizations, equipped with the power to provide for the global common good, the elimination of hunger and poverty and the sure defense of fundamental human rights. In this regard, I would also note the need for a reform of the United Nations Organization, and likewise of economic institutions and international finance, so that the concept of the family of nations can acquire real teeth."

This was a clear depiction of the Final World Empire embracing the Whore of Babylon. Moreover, of the wine in the cup of the Whore which is her teachings on the family of nations and the unifying of this world.

The Pope Embraces EU Federalism

The biggest shocker came on July 8, 2017, when the Pope embraced European Federalism. This aims for the unification of the European Union. World Federalism marches toward World government. The Pope stated during an interview with La Repubblica, "Europe needs to assume as soon as possible a federal structure. Either Europe becomes a federal community or otherwise it will count for nothing in the world."

The Pope's Criticism of the EU

A riff came when an EU Commission

internal document advised officials to use inclusive language such as "holiday season" and drop the word Christmas.

According to an article published November 2021 by Massimiliano Menichetti in Vatican news:

"Then, there is the cancellation of our roots, the Christian dimension of our Europe, especially with regard to Christian festivals. Of course, we know that Europe owes its existence and its identity to many influences, but we certainly cannot forget that one of the main influences, if not the main one, was Christianity itself. Therefore, destroying the difference and destroying the roots means precisely to destroy the person."

On December 2021, the Pope issued harsh words for the EU. Vatican News records:

"You refer to the European Union document on Christmas... this is an anachronism. In history many, many dictatorships have tried to do so. Think of Napoleon: from there... Think of the Nazi dictatorship, the communist one... it is a fashion of a watered-down secularism, distilled water... But this is something that throughout hasn't worked. … talking about the European Union, which I believe is necessary: the European Union must take in hand the ideals of the founding fathers, which were ideals of unity, of greatness, and be careful not to take the path of ideological colonization. This could end up dividing the countries and [causing] the European Union to fail. The European Union must respect each country as it is structured within, the variety of countries, and not want to make them uniform. … The European Union: its sovereignty, the sovereignty of brothers in a unity that respects the individuality of each country."

Pope Francis sees the European Union as necessary, and its vision of unity as in line with the Catholic churches. Although he is quick to criticize when the EU disregards Christian teachings or holidays. Midway during the Tribulation the Antichrist will turn on the Catholic Church. Moreover, on its teachings and persecute its followers. He will after plunder the Vatican and take its riches and churches.

5

AFRICA KING OF THE SOUTH

Jesus referenced the Queen of the South in two of the Gospels: Matthew 12:40 and Luke 11 31. When he mentioned the Queen of the South, he was referring to the Queen of Sheba who went and visited Solomon because she had heard of Solomon's wisdom. This famous Queen in the Old Testament is thought to have come from Ethiopia.

Candace Queen of Ethiopians

A second African queen is given a Biblical mention. In the book of Acts, we read of Candace the Queen of the Ethiopians. Acts 8: 26-29 tells the story of Philip being instructed to give the Gospel to her eunuch. Verse 27-28 describes, "So he arose and went. And behold, a man of Ethiopia, a eunuch of great authority under Candace the queen of the Ethiopians, who had charge of all her treasury, and had come to Jerusalem to worship, 28 was returning. And sitting in his chariot, he was reading Isaiah the prophet. Candace is thought to have reigned in the area of ancient Sudan, which is right next to Ethiopia.

King of the South in Daniel 11

In Daniel 11:40 a battle of the Antichrist is foretold with the King of the South. It reads: "At the time of the end the king of the South shall attack him; and the king of the North shall come against him like a whirlwind, with chariots, horsemen, and with many ships; and he shall enter the countries, overwhelm them, and pass through. We know that when Jesus is referring to the Queen of the South, he might be referencing what is today Ethiopia and Sudan. The Bible always views nations in their origins, and it can very well represent the continent of Africa today.

The African Union

Daniel 11:40 remained ambiguous until the

last couple of years. Africa was regarded as a third world continent in need of assistance from the nations of the world. Never was it seen as a possible fit for the Daniel 11:40 passage. Again, that is until recently.

The African Union formed in 2002 and joins all 55 member states of the African Continent. Prior to 2002 it existed as the Organization of African Unity, which originated in 1963 with a vision of a united Africa to eradicate colonialism or and apartheid.

The African Union on the other hand would aim to drive Africa's growth and economic development. Moreover, to accelerate the continent's political and economic integration. This included developing and promoting common policies on trade, defense, and foreign relations. Unifying aimed to ensure the defense of the Continent and the strengthening of its negotiating positions. The African Diaspora are invited to participate in the building of the African Union.

A Government

The African Union set up a governing body Its Union is based on treaties, and it established reforms and an agenda. The work of the AU is implemented through several principal decision-making organs: - The Assembly of Heads of State and Government, the Executive Council, the Permanent Representatives Committee (PRC), Specialized Technical Committees (STCs), the Peace and Security Council and The African Union Commission. The AU structure promotes participation of African citizens and civil society through the Pan-African Parliament and the Economic, Social & Cultural Council (ECOSOCC).

Organs that handle judicial and legal matters as well as human rights issues include: - African Commission on Human and Peoples' Rights (ACHPR), African Court on Human and Peoples' Rights (AfCHPR), AU Commission on International Law (AUCIL), AU Advisory Board on Corruption (AUABC) and the African Committee of Experts on the Rights and Welfare of the Child. The AU is also working towards the establishment of continental financial institutions (The African Central Bank, The African Investment Bank and the African Monetary Fund)

The Regional Economic Communities (RECs) and the African Peer Review

Mechanism are also key bodies that that constitute the structure of the African Union. In a nutshell the African Union is an integrated, prosperous, and peaceful Africa, driven by its own citizens and represents a dynamic force in the global arena.

The Union's Military

In November of 2011, the African Union set up The African Union-led Regional Task Force which is a multi-national military force in central Africa. It is authorized by the African Union's Peace and Security Council and approved by the UN as part of a Regional Co-operation Initiative for the elimination of the Lord's Resistance Army: a Ugandan rebel band.

African Union's Economic Growth

The African Union is no longer a third world wreck but is becoming its own market economy. According to the African Union Annual Economic Report:

Since the turn of the millennium, the growth accelerated across the entire continent and many countries frequently experienced annual double digit growth rates. In fact, the average growth rate is around 5% since 2000 while other regions have experienced a decline or a stagnation of their economic activity.

The EU and Africa

Of all the empires in our multipolar world, the European Union is most active in forming strong relations with the African Union that go beyond politics. Thus, the Africa of Bible prophecy has arrived on the scene. Moreover, it is forming relations with the European Union.

The heads of state or government of the member states of the African Union (AU) and the European Union (EU) met for the sixth European Union - African Union summit in Brussels on 17 and 18 February 2022. EU and AU leaders agreed on a joint vision for a renewed partnership.

The aims of the partnership are solidarity, security, peace and sustainable and sustained economic development and prosperity for the citizens of the two Unions. The leaders announced an Africa-Europe Investment Package of EUR 150 billion that will support a common ambition for 2030 and AU Agenda

2063. The investment package will help build more diversified, inclusive, sustainable, and resilient economies.

The leaders reaffirmed their commitment to work together to promote effective multilateralism within the rules-based international order, with the UN at its core. They pledged to work more closely together in multilateral fora to:

reduce global inequalities
strengthen solidarity
promote international cooperation
fight and mitigate climate change
improve delivery on 'global public goods', in line with the 2030 Agenda for Sustainable Development and AU Agenda 2063.

They committed to providing political support to achieve the necessary reform of the WTO and to improve its functioning to strengthen the multilateral trading system.

EU and African leaders also recommitted to the full implementation of the Paris Agreement and the outcomes of the COPs. They recognized that Africa's energy transition is vital for its industrialization and to bridge the energy gap. The EU will support Africa in its transition to foster just and sustainable pathways towards climate neutrality.

The EU has negotiated a series of economic partnership agreements (EPAs) with 48 countries in sub-Saharan Africa, within the framework of the Cotonou agreement. These agreements aim to create a shared trade and development partnership backed up by development support.

The African Union and the United States

In contrast to relations with the EU, the United States and the African Union in 2010, held their first high-level bilateral meeting in Washington. Its goal was to broaden the U.S.-AU relationship and deepen the level of engagement between both parties. The United States praised the AU for its peacekeeping efforts, especially in Darfur and Somalia; the United States also stated that it would rely on the AU to support global health and hunger initiatives. In 2011, the bilateral meetings identified youth engagement as a priority. In 2012, the two parties have put strong political pressure on Sudan and South Sudan to come to a solution over their shared border and interconnected economies.

The African Union and Russia

Concerning Russia and the African Union Paul Stronski in October 2019. Wrote in the Carnegie Endowment for International Peace:

Gradually, however, as the economy and domestic politics stabilized, and as the Kremlin's foreign policy horizons expanded, Russia began reestablishing a small foothold in Africa. In the mid-2000s, its outreach focused mainly on South Africa and the African Union—two entities it hoped could serve as partners to support its vision for a multipolar world. Russia then expanded its activities, buttressing its involvement in African peacekeeping operations and participating in the international anti-piracy task force off the coast of Somalia. Manifestations of increased Russian influence and presence in Africa have grown exponentially since. Relying on all instruments in its toolkit—political, military-security, economic, diplomatic, and informational—Russia has gamely sought to rebuild old ties and develop new ones.

What is interesting about Russia and the

African Union is that its policy is more ambitious than the United States and somewhat as aggressive as the European Union. The liaison of Russia and Africa might be the one spoken of in Daniel 11:40, as Russia is the king of the North.

China Africa

China has been Africa's largest trading partner since 2009 when it surpassed the United States and continues to be the largest trading partner as of 2020, albeit with a Coronavirus-induced drop in volume.

The need to protect China's increased investments in Africa has driven a shift away from China's traditional non-interference in the internal matters of other countries to new diplomatic and military initiatives to try to resolve unrest in South Sudan and Mali.

During the December 2015 FOCAC meeting in Johannesburg, South Africa, China's paramount leader Xi Jinping pledged $60 billion over three years in loans and assistance to the African continent. The stated aim of China's effort was to support factories manufacturing goods for export. Along with roads and ports, Nigerian President Muhammadu Buhari showed his desire to finish stalled railway projects along the coastline, specifically a 1,400 km railway from Lagos to Calabar representing approximately 200,000 jobs.

A 2020 report synthesizing close to a hundred studies on Africa-China economic relations finds that economic engagement with China supported Africa's economic transformation. At the same time, criticism against China has been growing from labor unions and civil society groups about the "poor labor conditions, unsustainable environmental practices, and job displacement" caused by Chinese enterprises. China is also thought to be taking advantage of African governments' weaknesses, thereby encouraging corruption and wasteful decision-making.

In addition, there are other negative stories circulating concerning China's involvement in Africa, which the EU would want to counter by its presence. It is noteworthy that in the last few years the EU has made Africa one of its major priorities. Its trade keeps increasing. But at the end of the Tribulation, the Antichrist will make some decisions toward the continent that will involve a battle that will also include Russia.

6

ISRAEL AND THE EU

Currently the European Union has an association agreement with Israel. It entered into force June 2000. It provides the legal and institutional framework for political dialogue and economic cooperation.

Israel is an Associated State of the European Union. These nations fulfill the economic and political requirements known as the Copenhagen criteria, which requires a candidate to have a democratic, free-market government together with the corresponding freedoms and institutions, and respect for the rule of law.

Therefore, this association agreement,

which already exists with Israel, provides the basis for the Antichrist's Treaty. But other developments have taken place to draw Israel closer to the EU.

The EU is Israel's largest trade market and accounts for about a third of Israel's total trade. Israel is the EU's most important trading partner in the Mediterranean area and was ranked as the EU's 24th trade partner globally in 2016. The most traded goods are chemicals and related products, machinery and transport equipment and manufactured goods.

Israel became a full partner in the Horizon 2020 Research Programme and benefitted from projects worth close to €170 million per year in the period 2017-2020. Since December 2021, Israel signed an Association Agreement to participate in the Horizon Europe Programme. These close associations provide the basis for the future all-encompassing peace that the Antichrist will provide Israel via the European Union.

Two State Solution

The European Union advocates a two-state solution regarding Israel and the Palestinians.

Yet, a two-state solution does not fit in with end time Bible Prophecy. Within this decade a shift is beginning to occur in EU Israel policy away from a two-state solution to a one state. This of course in preparation for the coming treaty that will be spearheaded by the Antichrist. Hugh Lovatt Senior Policy Fellow at the European Council on Foreign Relations, wrote on December 9, 2020, in his article, "The end of Oslo: A new European strategy on Israel-Palestine:"

"But, faced with Israel's consolidation of a one-state reality, public attitudes on both sides trending in opposite directions, and a shift in the political priorities of Arab states, the EU must at the very least acknowledge that it needs to adapt its strategy….But it will also do much to positively shift dynamics on the ground if it becomes apparent that it is already too late to sustain a viable and sovereign Palestinian state. Such a situation would require the two parties to work out how they can live with each other as equals preparing for a just one-state solution that provides meaningful stability and security to all."

"At the same time, Europeans must also make clear that, if Israel continues blocking a two-state solution, then the only other acceptable means of ensuring equal rights will be through a single democratic state…Ultimately, a European strategy centered on equality and deoccupation, rather than a dogmatic fixation on negotiations and the Oslo framework, is compatible with both a one-state and a two-state paradigm."

"… the EU's special representative for the Middle East Peace Process, Susanna Terstal. Indeed, during a hearing of the European Parliament's foreign affairs committee in July 2020, Terstal laid out the options: "There is only one alternative [to two states], that is one state … where two people live side by side with equal rights in peace and security."

We would expect to see a one state solution becoming more of the path pursued as the days move ahead toward the Ezekiel 38-39 war, which prompts the peace treaty that begins the Tribulation.

7

EU ARMY EMERGES

PESCO was written into the Lisbon Treaty It added the possibility for those members whose military capabilities with a view to the most demanding missions shall establish permanent structured cooperation (PESCO) within the EU framework. PESCO was seen as the way to enable the common defense foreseen in Article 42. It was termed, by President Jean-Claude Juncker, the Lisbon Treaty's "sleeping beauty."

On 7 September 2017, an agreement was made between EU foreign affairs ministers to move forward with PESCO with 10 initial projects. The agreement was signed on 13 November by 23 of the 28 member states. Ireland and Portugal notified the High Representative and the Council of the European Union of their desire to join PESCO on 7 December 2017. PESCO was activated by the 25 states on 11 December 2017 with the approval of a Council Decision.

NATO

About four-fifths of PESCO members are also member states of NATO. One EU state (Denmark) is a member of NATO but not a member of PESCO. While PESCO was formed in part due to doubts over the United States' commitment to NATO, officials stress that PESCO will be complementary to NATO security rather than in competition with it.

Strategic Compass

The EU is currently finalizing its Strategic Compass. This is its path to the boots on the ground for its army. In August of 2020 EU Defense ministers agreed at in informal meeting in Berlin to work on a common defense policy for Europe.

The EU's SIAC (Single Intelligence Analysis Capacity – consisting of EU Intelligence Centre and EU Military Staff Intelligence) thereafter prepared the first EU Threat

Analysis, based on input from the civilian and military intelligence services of the 27 EU Member States. The Threat Analysis covers threats and challenges that the EU and its Member States will face. This threat analysis is a classified document, not accessible to the public. So this is a secret EU report.

The Threat Analysis report paved the ground for the formulation of what is called the Strategic Compass. The Compass births EU armed forces for Common Security Defense Policy missions. It will develop a rapid deployment force of up to 5000 troops. It will invest in key miliary capabilities for land, sea, air, cyber and space.

 It will like other army's safeguard EU maritime security interests and deter and respond to cyber-attacks and foreign information manipulation. It will also strengthen cooperation with NATO, the UN, and OSCE, AU and ASEAN. Finally, it will boost cooperation with the US, Canada, Norway, and other countries.

According to Euractiv The document reads "We must act as a strong and coherent political actor to uphold the values and principles underpinning our democracies, support international peace and security and take more responsibility for the security of Europe and its citizens,".

Birth of Geopolitical Power

Due to the Russia Ukraine war, it just stepped up as a military power by offering weapons to Ukraine. Joseph Borrell the EU's High Representative of the EU for Foreign Affairs and Security Policy stated that the Ukraine war is now the birth of Geopolitical Europe. At this time EU bureaucrats and policy makers are discussing a new proposal to make a historic leap in the formation of the military by borrowing massive funds for this purpose. In addition, a European Security Council, in which the member nations would allow the Council to make decisions on their behalf for a common position and joint action.

The idea was first proposed by French President Emmanuel Macron in spring of 2019. It is again being proposed by a leading Europhile in the face of the Russia Ukraine war. While the EU's military infrastructure exists and its first troops will emerge, the Russian Ukraine war ignited a quantum leap for it becoming a military power overnight.

Antichrist's Army

The EU is the Revived Roman empire that will launch the Antichrist and this army will be used by him. We see this army in the siege of Jerusalem after the abomination of desolation. During the Tribulation the Antichrist will further refine it to become a crushing killing machine. We get a picture of this in Daniel 7:7: which states, "After this I saw in the night visions, and behold, a fourth beast, dreadful and terrible, exceedingly strong. It had huge iron teeth.: it was devouring, breaking in pieces, and trampling the residue with its feet.

We see in Isaiah 10:14 in the reference to the King of Assyria, which is a term for the Antichrist, "By the strength of my hand I have done it, And by my wisdom, for I am prudent; Also, I have removed the boundaries of the people, And have robbed their treasuries; so I have put down the inhabitants like a valiant man. My hand has found like a nest the riches of the people, And as one gathers eggs that are left, I have gathered all the earth; And there was no one who moved his wing, Nor opened his mouth with even a peep.

French Council Presidency

This year, on January 1, the French President took the helm of what is called the EU's Council of Minister's rotating presidency. Each member state gets a six-month term and France's last term was 13 years ago. In this presidency the function is to chair the meetings of the Council and determine its agenda. It sets a program that includes the other EU institutions.

French President Emmanuel Macron declared that his agenda is to render the EU a powerful Europe active in the world, fully sovereign, free in its choices and master of its own destiny. According to France 24 Macron stated, "The year 2022 must be a turning point for Europe." To mark this presidency France illuminated its historic buildings across the country in the blue of the EU flag and its stars including the Eiffel Tower and the Arc de Triomphe.

Macron made his EU Council Presidency a "moment to define the Strategic Compass." This is to finalize an EU army and give it its first troops by 2023 and fully operational by 2025.

Germany On Board

Not only is Emmanual Macron on board to boost the EU's military, on December 8, Olaf Scholz became Germany's new Chancellor. It was made it clear that the new government's coalition wants to use the ongoing Conference on the Future of Europe as a starting point for EU reform that should ultimately lead to the "development of a federal European state".

In sync with Emmanel Macron's vision, Germany not only wants to strengthen EU defense but its proposals also line with the idea of the EU breaking into an inner core with a group of states, again the beginning of what will be the ten-nation core we see in the books of Daniel and the Revelation. Scholz stated according to Oliver Noyan in his article in Euractiv, What Germany has in store for Europe in 2022. "We must always be prepared to try out solutions in groups of states if not all of them are ready yet, as we have already done with Schengen, with the euro or also in security and defense policy," he stated.

Not only did Macron have the support of Germany's chancellor who also has ambitious goals for the EU empire but also former ECB president Mario Draghi at the helm of Italy. The triad of motor nations want to build the EU into a strong empire helped push it forward closer to the Empire predicted in Scripture.

EU Army Infrastructure

I have talked about the EU army infrastructure as already in place. After several decades of evolution, the Lisbon Treaty of 2009 provided the structure that would be built upon. From the Common foreign and security policy to the European Defense Union to PESCO, Permanent Structured Cooperation. Think of both the EU's army and its currency the euro as having a backwards kind of formation that builds in layers from the bottom up.

Iron and Clay

Most other nations have built their armies from the top down, but due to the Unions complexity of so many nations represented in the iron and the clay of Daniel 2: 42-43 which reads: And as the toes of the feet were part of iron, and part of clay, so the kingdom shall be partly strong, and partly broken.
And whereas thou sawest iron mixed with miry

clay, they shall mingle themselves with the seed of men: but they shall not cleave one to another, even as iron is not mixed with clay. We see this even in the complicated building and rise of the EU world empire.

8

TEN NATIONS 3 PLUCKED

As I wrote in the Seat of the Antichrist, the European Union has been floating ideas for an inner core of members. This is because its government was never meant for 27 nations, but up to twelve maximums.

Enhanced Cooperation

The Lisbon Treaty of 2009 laid out put in a clause called, "enhanced cooperation." is a procedure where a minimum of nine EU member states are allowed to establish advanced integration or cooperation in an area within EU structures but without the other members being involved. Enhanced cooperation allows for a minimum of nine member states (which amounts to almost one-third) to co-operate within the structures of the EU without all member states. This allows them to move at different speeds, and towards different goals, than those outside the enhanced cooperation area. It is designed to overcome paralysis, where a proposal is blocked by the veto of an individual state or a small group who do not wish to be part of the initiative.

Schengen Agreement

Back in 1985 before the EU's major enlargement when consensus could not be reached among all EC member states on the abolition of border controls, five of the ten EEC member states agreed to go ahead as a group and abolish their borders. They signed the Schengen Agreement in the town of Schengen, Luxembourg. They established the Schengen Area separately from the European Economic Community.   The Schengen Convention of 1990 included the abolition of internal border controls and a common visa policy. Created in 1995 the Schengen Area adopted rules separate from the then European Community. The Schengen Treaties went onto become EU law and the inspiration for the approach to the inner core.

What is Enhanced Cooperation?

While Schengen provided the skeleton to the inner core of nations, enhanced cooperation provided the flesh on the bones. It also unfolded Bible Prophecy and provides a path to its fulfillment. Enhanced Cooperation will lead to ten nation federation

Enhanced Cooperation needs a minimum of nine Member States, who file a request with the European Commission. This is no coincident that nine is the minimum number. We know this will lead to the ten.

Macron's coalition of ten in Defense provides the Biblical number and sets a precedent.

The ten-nation federation of Prophecy will occur in the EU Council. Based on the predictions in the book of Daniel and Revelation and understanding how the EU works, this change will occur in the EU Council. What the Bible shows us is the final world empire's governmental institutional structure. This lines perfectly with the

European Union's. Except that there are 28 members in the Council, but in the future, it will break into this inner core and we will see ten.

Fundamental Law

In 2010 Andrew Duff founded the Spinelli Group named after his mentor. As a fellow EU builder Andrew Duff would help ensure the EU would evolve along the same federalist path and this is the purpose of the Spinelli group. As a European Federalist Andrew Duff is also a leading figure in the EU's liberal left parties. In addition to helping find the Spinelli group, Andrew Duff is also president of the European Union of Federalists and a founding member of the ECFR: European Council on Foreign Relations.

Andrew Duff is currently helping to forge the EU's future. He wrote the outline and oversaw the drafting of A Fundamental Law Treaty to amend Lisbon and all previous EU treaties, which will give the EU a full-fledged federal government. Proposals that were drafted by members of the EU Parliament and others have now been concluded at the Conference on the Future of Europe and will make it into EU policy. I interviewed Mr. Duff in 2015 concerning enhanced cooperation and this is a portion of the dialogue.

Erika Grey

It is very unclear in the treaty, in the Fundamental Law

Andrew Duff

I think it has to be tried a lot more than it has been tried up to now.

Erika Grey

But will there be two chambers when those nations go forward?

Andrew Duff

Yes. Essentially

Erika Grey

Will there be one chamber in the council and then you mentioned the associate members as well, so does it become a three tier, or does it become three circles where you have the inner core. Then you have your union, and then you have the associate members.

Andrew Duff

Yes, I mean I see that the reinforced cooperation clauses of the Lisbon treaties as all being about Multi Speed Europe, so that all Member States agree on the direction, but they can't all get there and are not prepared to get there at the same time. The associate affiliation of a second-class Member State, which is what we're taking about with respect to the UK, if it wishes to go there is of a qualitatively not the same thing. It's a parking place. And it could either be a short-term parking place or a long-term parking place depending on the political will and circumstances that prevail at any one time.

EU Parliament Draft Report

The Draft The Committee on Constitutional Affairs first published this draft in July of 2016 and issued further amendments in November, The draft talks about integrating the European Council into what would be called a Council of States and replace the six-month rotating presidency with "a system of permanent chairs chosen from their midst: It suggests that the idea of creating a special law Council should be favorably considered. The special law council might would fit the 10 kings along with the Antichrist picture in Bible Prophecy.

Reimagine Europa

Reimagine Europa was formed by the now diseased former French President Valery Giscard d'Estaing. Its purpose is to help to create a smaller Europe that will go forward with 12 members. For more information see Valéry Giscard d'Estaing: Toward a smaller Europe.

Draft Report Amendments

The inner core of members continued to be floated around in varying degrees within the European Union. In 2016 nation EU Parliament Draft Report on possible evolutions of and adjustments to the current institutional set-up of the European Union by the Committee on Constitutional Affairs wrote a draft report and issued further amendments in November.

EU Council of States

The draft talks about integrating the European Council into what would be called a Council of States and replace the six-month rotating presidency with "a system of permanent chairs chosen from their midst suggests that the idea of creating a special law Council should be favorably considered. The special law council might would fit the 10 kings along with the Antichrist picture in Bible Prophecy.

It also recommends that, instead of these multiple derogations, a type of 'associate status,' could be proposed to those states in the periphery that only want to participate on the sideline, i.e., in some specific Union policies; this status should be accompanied by obligations corresponding to the associated rights.

Notes that, despite the prohibition in Article 15(1) TEU, the European Council has undertaken various legislative initiatives; proposes abolishing Article 15(1) and integrating the European Council into a Council of States that could engage legitimately in the law-making process and provide direction and coherence to the other specialized Council configurations.

Considers that this Council and its specialized configurations, as the second chamber of the EU legislature, should, in the interest of specialism, professionalism and continuity, replace the practice of the rotating six-month presidency with a system of permanent chairs chosen from their midst; suggests that the idea of creating a special Law Council should be favorably reconsidered.

Emmanuel Macron 10 Nation Coalition

In May 2018 Emmanuel Macron ignited Bible Prophecy boards when he suggested to bring together a 10-nation coalition of the willing. According to Paul Taylor for Politico EU this was: "designed to prepare European armed forces to take action together in emergencies, and to bind Britain into military cooperation as it leaves the EU….

Frustrated by the big-tent, low-ambition start to the European Union's so-called Permanent Structured Cooperation (PESCO) in defense agreed last year at Germany's insistence, the French leader is pressing ahead with a small core of like-minded nations outside EU and NATO institutional structures.

Iron Legs and Toes

Some Bible Prophecy teachers' mis identify the legs and toes on Nebuchadnezzar's dream image (Daniel 2: 31-41), which symbolizes the four kingdoms and relates their strength to metals. The golden head of the image is Babylon. Its silver arms and chest are the Medes and Persians. Its bronze thighs represent the Greek empire, and its legs and feet are of iron, but the toes have clay mingled in with the iron. Biblical scholars assume the image has ten toes when the Bible does not provide the number of toes. On the two legs, the identities range from the Byzantine, east from west division to a depiction of the EU merging with the Islamic nations. Then there are the teachings it is the Ottomans and not the Roman empire at all. The two legs represent the division of the ten kings, which is one leg to the remaining kings on the other leg, which make up this power's government.

When the Bible depicts the final world empire, there are no more references to past empires, this is the revived Empire in its final form. We can now know the certain representation of the two legs with the empire before us in its early stages Thus ten toes are on one foot and the remaining nations on the other depicting the remaining nations.

Three Nations Plucked up by the Roots

In unison with the ten horns in the book of Daniel we read of the three horns plucked up by the roots. The following passages record:

Daniel 7:7…It was different from all the beasts that were before it, and it had ten horns.

8 I was considering the horns, and there was another horn, a little one, coming up among them, before whom three of the first horns were plucked out by the roots.

Daniel 7:19 …and the ten horns that were on its head, and the other horn which came up, before which three fell, namely, that horn which had eyes and a mouth which spoke pompous words, whose appearance was greater than his fellows.

The Mystery Is No More

At the writing of the *Seat of the Antichrist* there were no correlations or possibilities in geopolitics on how this verse would be fulfilled. This changed this last decade with the Visegrad nations. The Visegrad Group (also known as the Visegrad Four, the V4, or the European Quartet) is a cultural and political alliance of four Central and Eastern European countries: the Czech Republic, Hungary, Poland, and Slovakia.

These nations have brought the EU a considerable amount of grief, especially Hungary. They advocate a confederation vs a federation, and are right wing leaning, and oppose many of the EU's policies such as on Migration. According to Euractiv in December of 2018 EU Council President Charles Michel suggested the Visegrad nations be ousted out of the Schengen area. The article states: "Hungarian PM Viktor Orbán, the most flamboyant exponent of the anti-immigration position of the four Visegrad countries (Hungary, Poland, Czech Republic, and Slovakia), told journalists the debate on migration had been stormy. He also said that the last attempt to impose rules on how to run migration had failed."

Rule of Law Procedure Against Hungary

DW reported that the EU triggered a rule of law procedure against Hungary in April of 2022 for breaching the EU's democratic standards. This legal tool which was never used before could strip Hungary of its EU funding.

This past decade the Visegrad nations and their political parties have caused a good deal of grief for Europhiles. Most likely it is among these nations that three will be uprooted from the European Union. It is the membership of these nations that effects the EU moving forward. It is amazing how as time passes the fig tree ripens more and more. So much so that we can see their correlation to the prophetic forecasts.

9

FALL OF US RISE OF EU EMPIRE

Donald Trump Presidency

There was no US president more responsible for the EU moving forward into an empire than Donald Trump. He served as the United States's 45th president from January 20, 2017, until January 20, 2021. According to Alice Tidey in "How did US President Donald Trump impact Europe during his four years in office, which appeared in Euronews:

"During his presidency, Trump publicly snubbed or berated European allies — seemingly refusing to shake Angela Merkel's hand at the White House — but cozied up to long-time foes — he described Vladimir Putin as a "terrific person" and Kim Jong-Un as a "great leader".

He also pulled out or threatened to pull out of international treaties or institutions promoting a rules-based global order. Washington withdrew from the Paris Agreement on climate change and from the landmark nuclear deal with Iran and initiated the process to pull out of the World Health Organization (WHO) during a global pandemic. Trump also fustigated the World Trade Organization (WTO) and NATO."

This allowed the EU to put a leading footprint on the World Health Organization and the World Economic Forum. Moreover, Trump's policy's added impetus to the cause for the completion of a European Army.

60th Anniversary of the Treaty of Rome

The 60th anniversary of the **Treaty of Rome** became a turning point for European Union politicians. They declared a renewed commitment to the European project. While I attended the 60th anniversary of the Treaty of Rome in Rome at a Spinelli event, I listened to

EU power weight and federalist Elmar Brok state among other names of the populist right that Donald Trump and the other named are the founders of the New Europe It was the first time that Europe could not rely on its partner. It drove on the fence European politicians to the cause of EU unity and strength. The insurrection at the US capital provided the cement and glue for the European view.

Punching up to its Weight

Just prior to Donald Trump's Presidency the EU started to punch up to its weight. It sits on the largest to second largest market depending on the report, and about a half a billion citizens. It is nearly a third larger than the United States. Around 2014 the EU under Commissioner Margrethe Vestager, in charge of competition policy investigated Facebook's acquisition of WhatsApp. Facebook ended up with a fine of a whopping 110 million euro fine for violating the EU's merger policy. Several other US big tech companies were fined for violating various EU antitrust regulations.

The astronomical fines were larger than EU member states paid into the EU budget.

According to CNBC, Google was fined a combined 9.5 billion euros in 2017, Apple was ordered to pay back Ireland 14.5 billion euros for past taxes. Bloomberg reported that Amazon was hit with a record 865 million euros for violating the EU's data-protection rules. The decision was triggered by a 2018 complaint from a French privacy group. The EU was now flexing its muscles.

Rewriting Rules for the World

Columbia Law professor Anu Bradford a citizen of both the US and Finland authored, "The Brussels Effect: How the European Union Rules the World" published February 25, 2020. It provides her analysis of the European Union's outside influence on global issues, including antitrust law, data privacy, food safety, and climate change.

The EU changed websites around the globe with its General Data Protection Regulation (GDPR), which governs how personal data of individuals in the EU may be processed and transferred. This went into effect on May 25, 2018. All websites now have a notification and requests your permission.

The European Union went much further than GDPR. Its Digital Services Act (DSA) rewrote the rules for the internet. It targeted e-Commerce illegal content, transparent advertising, and disinformation. It would require the big social networks to act as publishers and verify information.

At the same time came the EU's Digital Markets Act (DMA) It addresses the negative consequences arising from platforms acting as digital "gatekeepers" to the internal market. These are platforms that have the power to act as private rule-makers and that can function as bottlenecks between businesses and consumers. When Twitter banned Donald Trump because his claims of election fraud were not verifiable, other platforms acted in unison. These actions were prompted by the EU's new laws for the internet. His claims of election fraud were not verified.

On 22 April 2022, European policymakers reached an agreement on the Digital Services Act. The final stage before the two bills come into law is the vote by representatives of the individual parliaments and policymakers from the 27 member nations, which is a formality.

World Regulator of AI

The European Union's rewriting of rules did not stop there. In April 2021, the European Commission released its 108-page proposal to regulate artificial intelligence ("AI"), describing it as an attempt to ensure a "well-functioning internal market for artificial intelligence systems" that is based on "EU values and fundamental rights." It is the bloc's first major attempt to comprehensively regulate such systems, and will have global repercussions

The Battery Directive

In March 2022 The proposal for a regulation concerning batteries and waste batteries, which would replace the 2006 Batteries Directive would govern the entire battery lifecycle. It would establish mandatory requirements for sustainability (such as carbon footprint rules, minimum recycled content, performance and durability criteria), safety and labelling for the marketing and putting into service of batteries, and requirements for end-of-life management. It would also introduce due diligence obligations for economic operators sourcing raw materials. The proposed regulation could provide a blueprint for further initiatives under the EU sustainable product policy, aimed at making sustainable products the norm.

Companies around the world would not be able to sell their batteries to the European Union if they did not conform to the European Union's standards.

While the world was not paying attention, and still considering the European Union a failed project that would fall apart, it was rewriting various rules for the world. The European Union was punching up to its weight and this is only the beginning.

COVID 19 Pandemic

The EU adopted the European Green Deal to act as a lifeline out of the COVID-19 pandemic and its economic impact. It would beat the United States to the punch on Climate policy, which promised a boost to its economy. The US's market will trail behind by two years. In part because it pulled out of the Paris Climate Accords While COVID-19 decimated the economies of the world it acted as another vehicle to help build the EU empire.

Fines on US Tech Companies and CO2

As part of the EU's recover it issued bonds and pay for these in part by taxes on US tech companies and CO2 violators who violate their climate rules. The US ranks high in these breaches and its corporations would be paying into the EU recovery. Recently with the high gas prices because of the Russian Ukraine war, the EU wants to give subsidies to citizens. These will be paid for via energy taxation which will most likely include monies from US companies. Hearing these proposals coming from Brussels among others should have had American's hair standing on end.

Joe Biden Presidency

When Joe Biden became president in January 2021, he let it be known to the world that America was back. Former President Obama during his inauguration stated that America was not in first place anymore in the World and that Biden was one who could deal with these challenges. Joe Biden's strength was foreign policy, which was why Obama chose him as Vice President. On Bidne's first overseas trip to Europe in June 2021 that included meetings with the Group of Seven and NATO leaders, the European Union let it be known that they were forging ahead with their own interests.

Biden upset Europeans when he met with Vladimir Putin and did not include EU leaders. The EU was ready to forge with a big investment pact with China and omitted the United States. The view concerning Biden across the Atlantic was one of mistrust. The nation was considered unreliable because of their election of Donald Trump. They considered that he might get reelected. In addition to putting in the power of the presidency someone of the same ilk.

Decline of the Dollar Rise of the Euro

Russia took a swipe at the dollar when the first set of US sanctions were issued in response to Russia invading Crimea in 2014. After the Countering America's Adversaries Through Sanctions Act of 2017, in which Russia was added, more sanctions were issued. In the face of these Russia began moving away from the dollar. In addition, other sanctioned nations and China joined the actions. Along with Turkey, Iran, India and Brazil. . According to Alexy Lossan in his article Why Rare Russia and China Ditching the US dollar? Published in Russia Beyond on September 4, 2020:

In 2019, Russia and China signed a treaty to use national currencies in mutual trading. This added to the gradual reduction in the dollar's traffic - from 90 percent in 2015 to only 46 percent so far in 2020… the Russian Central Bank has been consistently reducing the U.S. dollar share in its reserves.

In April 2018, following the new round of stringent U.S. sanctions, Russia expedited the withdrawal of its reserves out of U.S. government bonds. Russian investments into them fell by half - from $96.1 billion to $48.7 billion in May, and then once more, to $14.9 billion. For comparison, in February 2013, during a peak period (and before the reunification with Crimea), Russian investments in U.S. bonds totaled $164.3 billion.

These actions continued and were so extreme and effective that when Russia was hit by a landslide of Western Sanctions in the face of the Russia Ukraine war, the value of the Ruble increased.

EU moves from dollars to euros in energy transactions

In. December 2018 the EU Commission enacted a recommendation for EU member states to move from US dollars in their energy transactions and to report to the Commission on their progress yearly. This was in response to US sanctions on Iran that effected German companies The (European Stability Mechanism) is a funding program for Eurozone members established by a treaty.

Economist Elina Ribakova who writes for Bruegel a highly regarded economic think tank, which EU politicians consult for economic policy decisions stated in her article, How the EU could transform the energy market: The case for a euro crude-oil benchmark:

"There is a strong case for an oil benchmark in euros. Trading energy markets in more than one currency is not unprecedented, and indeed used to be the norm. Europe – with its powerful currency and reliable regulatory environment – should stand a good chance of success."

A blog post written on the ESM blog by Kalin

Anev Janse who is the chief financial officer of the ESM and management board member. He previously worked in strategy at the European Investment Bank in Luxembourg. He wrote last on how the Euro is now favored by Central Banks compared to several years ago. The greatest shocker came on the eve of Joe Biden's inauguration in January 2020. The European Commission called for the euro to become the global reserve currency and set a plan in motion to achieve that end. Moreover, for a multipolar international monetary system vs a dollar dominated one and in which the euro is an opted for reserve currency.

US Debt Capital Markets Banking Union

US debt is now at nearly 31 trillion dollars and the United States keeps piling on more. The website Truth in Accounting puts the figure at 142 trillion dollars. Given the rate of American debt which is now a whopping 103% of GDP, once the EU completes its Capital Market's Union and Banking Union it will most likely be the final straw to topple the US dollar.

EU's Hedged Economy

The EU has a hedged economy. During this

last decade it concluded one trade agreement after the other. Several breaking records in their scope. These total about 84 while the United States only amount to 20. When the US dollar tanks, the EU economy will be hedged. At one time the EU indices followed the USs, and they are no longer running in sync. Not to mention the EU is also adding association agreements These agreements alone will render the EU more powerful and prosperous than the United States and China because it extends its reach throughout the Globe. When you add that its Green recovery plan and it is changing the rules of the world in its favor along with its investment in game changing products, the sky is the limit.

The Beast of Revelation

Revelation 18 lists all the products of the final world empire. The passage along with Jeremiah 51 and others established the empire as a place of trade. Ezekiel 16: 29 confirms, "Moreover you multiplied your acts of harlotry as far as the land of the trader, Chaldea; and even then, you were not satisfied. "The Word of God's accuracy is amazing and as was stated, "The Scriptures prove themselves." The EU is to the letter as described

Now the Beast is swimming in the water and has not yet come out of the sea. This will occur at its height of power and under the coming ten king inner core of members.

10
FINAL AGE OF EMPIRES

The Russia Ukraine war caused a major geopolitical tectonic shift. George Bush's new world order of international rules with US supremacy, which had been in the dust pin of history for some time, was finally realized by Evangelicals. Many of them embroiled in the false teachings of a great reset to be ushered in by elites and secret societies for world government were stymied by the events.

The prophet Daniel in fact forecast an age of empires as the geopolitical order that will be in place at the time of the end. The book of Daniel and Revelation does not describe a world order conspired for by elites. Moreover, the Biblical books specify a powerful empire ruling. In addition to the Scriptures mention of other empires and nations.

Age of Empires

Geopolitically we live in what is called a multipolar world. EU Power politician Guy Verhofstadt who I met in Rome at the 60th Anniversary of the Treaty of Rome, coined it perfectly in 2009 when he called it "an age of empires." On Sept 16, 2019, he stated again that "the world order of tomorrow is not a world based on nation states or countries. It's a world order that is based on empires."

In his speech he references the US and Russia as empires and that the only way that Europe will be able to defend its interests is by doing it together, other words within the EU empire. We also see the rise of the African Union another upcoming empire mentioned in Daniel 11 as the King of the South.

In May of 2022 Euractiv reported that German Chancellor Olaf Scholz traveled to Africa "to forge closer ties with like-minded democracies in an increasingly multipolar world order currently being reshaped by Russia's war in Ukraine." Berlin sees Africa as crucial to ensure the stability of the global rules-based order further evidencing the EU's relations with who the book of Daniel describes as the King of the South. Not to mention that this empire has only recently come to the level of power for such recognition.

Currently in this empire age we see each of the empires jockeying for position. This includes the United States. The US is desperately trying to hang on to the unipolar world it ruled, but its reign is over. Moreover, when the US dollar crashes it will drop the US out of the end time power line up.

End of Globalization

Economists and other experts started to write in 2019 that globalization was ending. The COVID-19 pandemic showed the disunity of the world order. It became every nation for themselves. The final nail in the coffin of globalization was the Russia Ukraine war. During which Arnab from India's largest news outlet affirmed that we are in an order where every empire or nation must look after their own interests. Several media outlets reported on BlackRock's CEO Larry Fink's comment that the Russia Ukraine war is upending the world order and that it ushered in the end of globalization. Wall Street now warned of globalization's end.

Globalization's demise has also stymied the end time prophecy channels who relied on it for their erroneous conspiracies of their one world government within a new world order. This is despite the many details given in the book of Daniel of a final empire age.

Regionalization

While Vladimir Putin was in China meeting with Xi Xing Ping finalizing a gas deal and their common stand against the West, the EU was meeting with the African Union. Unbeknownst to many prophecy watchers, the world moved away from globalization and the rules based international institutions are not as effective. It is becoming regionalized, meaning when Russia united with China, these two empires regionalized and formed a bullwork against the Western empires. The US then aligned with the EU and was welcomed for this reason.

Russia united with China and India, while the EU united with the US, Canada and the UK, with both having other smaller nations. The Russian group are moving away from the US dollar. Thus, this is not just causing a political split but economic as well. US and EU sanctions are also contributing to the regional division.

EU Empire Expanding

The EU Parliament held an emergency session where the Ukraine asked to join the EU. Georgia and Moldovia followed. The Russia Ukraine war lent to even greater expansion of the EU empire. French President Emmanuel Macron called for a "European Political Community" which would be spearheaded by the EU and include non-EU countries. According to Schengenvisainfo News on May 10, 2022, Macron stated:

"This new European organization would allow the democratic European nations adhering to our core values to find a new area of political cooperation, security, cooperation in energy, transport, investment, infrastructure, movement of people and especially our youth," he said."

Considering the nations clamoring for EU

membership, the proposal ads to all the European Union's various association agreements and trade pacts. This reveals the potential for the European Union's reach.

Leap in Military

The EU made a historic leap in the formation of their military by borrowing massive funds for this purpose. In addition to adding a European Security Council, in which the member nations would allow the Council to make decisions on their behalf for a common position and joint action. The idea was first proposed by French President Emmanuel Macron in spring of 2019. It is again being proposed by a leading Europhile in the face of the Russia Ukraine war.

Therefore, the face of the new world order has now emerged as one of empires. The EU Empire is writing many rules now for the world. If nations do not comply with their internet policy, theirs on AI and Climate, they will not be able to trade with this vast empire. Concurrently with this Russian Ukraine war, pro EU Emmanuel Macron led the Council Presidency and EU power politician Guy Verhofstadt steered the Conference on the

Future of Europe for Treaty Changes to a more political and powerful empire.

Treaty Change

The Conference on the Future of Europe concluded, and it was decided to do away with the EU's unanimity rule. This means votes must be unanimous for major policy to go forward. This rule held back a lot of decisions that would render the EU a powerful empire. This will now be done away with.

One of the proposals was for the EU to act as "a strong actor on the world scene in peace."
It also advocates that the EU play "a leading role in building the world security order after the war in Ukraine. In addition, it aims for the EU to "as a strong actor on the world scene in relationship building." And to "make greater use of its collective political and economic weight, speaking with one voice and acting in a unified way, without individual Member States dividing the Union through inappropriate bilateral responses"

On trade it recommends that the EU promote sustainable and rules-based trade while opening new trade and investment opportunities for European companies. In addition, that it concludes major international cooperation agreements as the EU rather than as individual countries42.

For Europe to Lead the World in Digital Transformation

The proposals did not stop with trade. It stated, "Europe must become a world leader and standard setter in digital transformation and charter a European way to build an ethical, human-centered, transparent, and safe digital society." Another words the EU must lead the world in all areas.

Sanction Policy

Like the US it calls for the EU To strengthen its ability to sanction States, governments, entities, groups, or organizations. In addition, adding individuals who do not comply with its fundamental principles, agreements, and laws. They want to and ensure that sanctions that already exist are quickly implemented and enforced. Sanctions against third countries should be proportional to the action that triggered them and be effective and applied in due.

The Russia Ukraine war revealed frightening implications of sanction policy. Imagine how this will be used in a future dictatorship against all kinds of people. We know it will occur against those who do not take the Mark of the Beast.

Still no Democratic Legitimacy

While there were proposals for the EU decision making process, such as recommending that the Council of the EU could be called the Senate of the EU. Moreover, the European Commission could be called the Executive Commission of the EU. Nevertheless, there is no change in the EU's undemocratic institutional structure. It was suggested that MEPs be voted on transnational lists and a more democratic process for the Commission President election. These were not concretely written as other proposals. Moreover, they do not fix the European Union's democratic deficit, which is key in the Antichrist's ability to take control of the EU system for dictatorial power.

A Frighting Time

We are in a frightening time right now. This

past decade the empire went forward and yet it remained virtually invisible in the process. My YouTube channel and articles were barely viewed because my message was ahead of its time. Moreover, I have been speaking on the multipolar world, empire age that was evolving for some time now. Soon the reality of this new empire order will become apparent not only to those in leadership but to the world's citizens.

Sadly, the Evangelical world was looking for conspiracies and other fiction. They dominated the Evangelical airwaves. The building of the empire remained invisible to the world, but the developments were being broadcast on my channel and in my books and articles. It was as if a blindness was over the evolving empire to protect it and ensure it would move forward. It prompted me to ask in my interview with Andrew Duff the European Union's constitutional specialist, one of the EU architects and a leading figure in the European Movement, who I cited earlier in this book this question in 2015.

Erika Grey
European federalism is misunderstood in Europe. Virtually unheard of in the United

States, and yet federalism is the ideology that drives the European Union and many EU federalists held and hold leading positions in EU institutions. Why do you think that with such a sophisticated and educated group of adherents to the ideology, which includes journalists is European federalism misunderstood within the EU nations and virtually unheard of around the world?

Andrew Duff

"It's an extremely good question and I ask myself that a lot…"

This is not the case anymore. This European Union, the final world empire has emerged. It is also beginning to show that it is a bully, who is making other nations conform to its rules via trading with its market. This might also be how the Mark of the Beast goes global, if it is not used, there will be no trading with the Empire. By that time, we can only imagine the number of trade pacts and discoveries for which it will take the lead that will greatly prosper it.

The world has just changed, and we are clearly in the empire age predicted by the prophet Daniel, with the lineup of nations mentioned in the book. The United States does not have the power alone to meet up to the challenges of this new order. But when the United States dollar ceases to be the world's reserve the US will enter a major crisis. It will remain a great nation but no longer a leading one. As I stated in the Seat of the Antichrist, it will have no choice but to follow the lead of the EU and be in league with it

Exceedingly Strong, Dreadful and Terrible.

It will be exactly as the prophet Daniel predicted it. An empire that is exceedingly strong, dreadful, and terrible.

Daniel 7;7 states, "After this I saw in the night visions, and behold, a fourth beast, dreadful and terrible, exceedingly strong. It had huge iron teeth; it was devouring, breaking in pieces, and trampling the residue with its feet. It was different from all the beasts that were before it, and it had ten horns.

This is what is coming a terrifying empire and we are already beginning to see its strength and how it is using its power. As it adds more nations and trade agreements and makes its final changes it will be greater in scope than

China and the US combined.

Moreover, we can only imagine the rules it will make for the world once the Antichrist is at the helm and changes times and laws. Seeing this empire come to fruition should have us in both awe and fright. Its not a new world order run by conspirators, its an empire, an extremely strong and powerful one and we have seen it develop and begin to rise. We also see its potential from here.

We are now in the final empire age the book of Daniel predicted. Not to mention there will be no need for me to write a follow up to this book. You will find those details in the Scriptures, in the book of Daniel and the Revelation. There will of course be the finishing touches on the empire, the finalization of policy discussed in this book. But, by the time it should be written about I will have been Raptured out of this earth. This book will act as confirmation for the Tribulation Saints. Next of course will be the arrival of the Antichrist.

Final Thoughts

. If there was ever any proof that is needed that

the Words of the Bible are real, it is in these pages. The Bible says to believe on the name of the Lord Jesus Christ, and you will be saved. This is the only hope for those of us who are seeing these events occur as they were predicted.

We are the lucky ones because we will be Raptured out of this world just prior to the start of the Tribulation. This is our additional hope. If you are reading this now you will not want to be here during the Tribulation, when the greatest empire of all ages, the final world empire, which is the European Union will essentially be ruling the world under the Antichrist.

But for those who will not come to know Christ except during the Tribulation, He is their hope as well because their days are literally numbered, but at the end, Jesus is their prize and eternal life with Him. Revelation 12:11 states, And they overcame him by the blood of the Lamb and by the word of their testimony and they loved not their lives unto death.

I can attest that will all my years of study, research, and interviews, it all fits perfectly like a puzzle. The Scriptures in fact prove themselves. This work will not conclude with the invitation of Jesus in the Revelation.

Jesus states in Revelation 3: 20-21:

"Behold, I stand at the door and knock. If anyone hears My voice and opens the door, I will come in to him and dine with him, and he with Me.

To him who overcomes I will grant to sit with Me on My throne, as I also overcame and sat down with My Father on His throne.

Also in Revelation 22:16-17:

"I, Jesus, have sent My angel to testify to you these things in the churches. I am the Root and the Offspring of David, the Bright and Morning Star."

And the Spirit and the bride say, "Come!" And let him who hears say, "Come!" And let him who thirsts come. Whoever desires, let him take the water of life freely.

ABOUT THE AUTHOR

Erika Grey, author, Bible scholar, commentator, journalist has been a born-again Christian for over 40 years She has written numerous books on Bible Prophecy and made contributions in helping to decode the more difficult forecasts. She has spoken on numerous radio stations including Coast to Coast.

This book is one of a series of short books by Erika Grey intended to be quick reads with important information. Be sure to check out Erika's other titles at www.erikagrey.com.